MAHABHARATA STORIES

Living in Exile

Subhadra Sen Gupta

Om Books International

As the Pandavas walked through the streets of Hastinapur on their way to exile, the people of the kingdom came out to bid them farewell. Many were upset, others filled with sorrow because they all wanted Yudhishthira to be their king.

Leaving them behind, the Pandavas and Draupadi entered the forest and began to live there for the first twelve years of their banishment. Many rishis lived with them. Lord Krishna often visited them as they planned to get back their kingdom.

Their most difficult time was when twelve years of exile were over. Now the Pandavas had to live in hiding for one year and if they were discovered, their exile would go on for another twelve years.

Arjuna said to his brothers, “We have to disguise ourselves as ordinary people and not of royal blood and not behave like warriors.” Sahadev nodded, “Yes. We have to leave the forest and work in another kingdom.”

They arrived at the palace of King Virata, who ruled over the kingdom of Matsya. King Virata was a powerful ruler and was not afraid of Duryodhana. Yudhishthira went and bowed before the king.

Yudhishthira said, “Your Majesty, we are five Brahmins who are looking for work. We pray to you to let us serve you in the palace.” King Virata who did not recognise the Pandavas as they were dressed as Brahmins, asked, “What kind of work can you do?”

Yudhishthira said, “I have worked in the court of kings as a trusted courtier and I can also play dice.” Then he pointed to Draupadi and said, “My wife is experienced in working in the palaces of royal women.”

Bhima said, “I am a good cook and can present delicious dishes at your feast.”

Arjuna who was dressed as a woman said, “I am a dancer and can teach the princesses dance and music.”

Nakul said, “I am a good rider and I love horses and driving chariots.”

And Sahadev said, “I can work in the cattle sheds and take care of your cows.”

Yudhishthira assumed the name of Kanka and became a companion to King Virata, playing dice with him. As he was a wise man, he also advised the king on matters of the court.

Draupadi now called herself Sairandhari and began to work as Queen Sudeshna's maid, helping her dress and style her hair.

Bhima took the name of Ballava and began to work in the palace kitchen and gathered praises for his cooking.

Arjuna dressed as a woman and called himself Brihannala. He began teaching Princess Uttara, the daughter of King Virata, to dance.

Nakul as Damagranthi worked in the stables, feeding and training the horses of Virata's army.

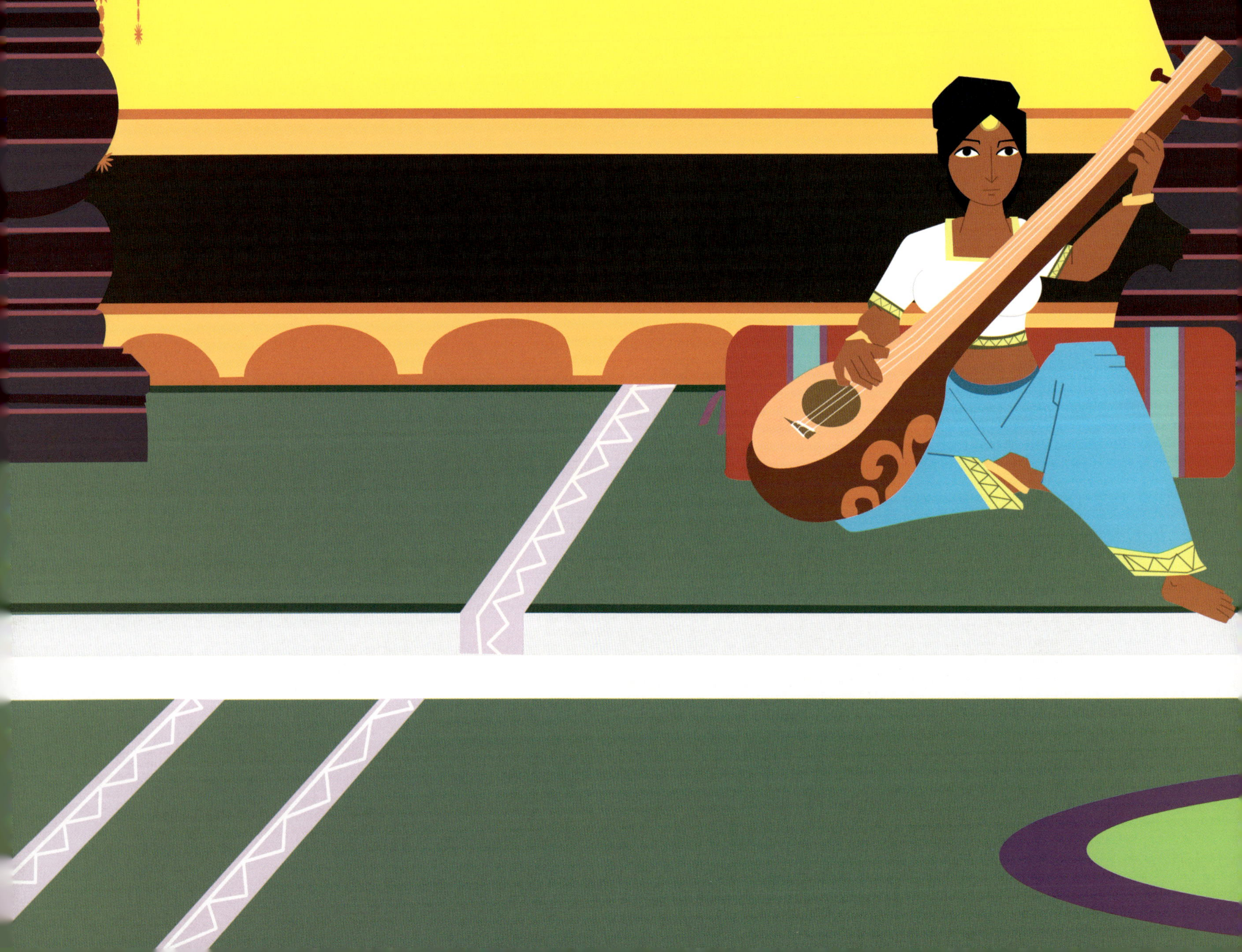

Sahadev was now called Tantipala and he worked in the cowshed, feeding and milking hundreds of cows.